WRITERS' WORKSHOP

on becoming a writer

Audrey Gregory
Judy Keiner
Heather Lyons
Angela Redfern

tb

Trentham Books

First published in 1991 by Trentham Books

Trentham Books
Unit 13/14
Trent Trading Park
Botteslow Street
Stoke-on-Trent ST1 3LY

British Library Catlaloguing in Publication Data

Writers' Workshop: on becoming a writer
Gregory, Audrey
    Writers' Workshop in the Classroom
    1. Writing, Language, Schools, primary
    I. Title. II. Keiner, Judith. III. Lyons, Heather. IV Redfern, Angela
    410.7

ISBN 0 948080 37 X

Printed by The Bemrose Press, Chester

CONTENTS

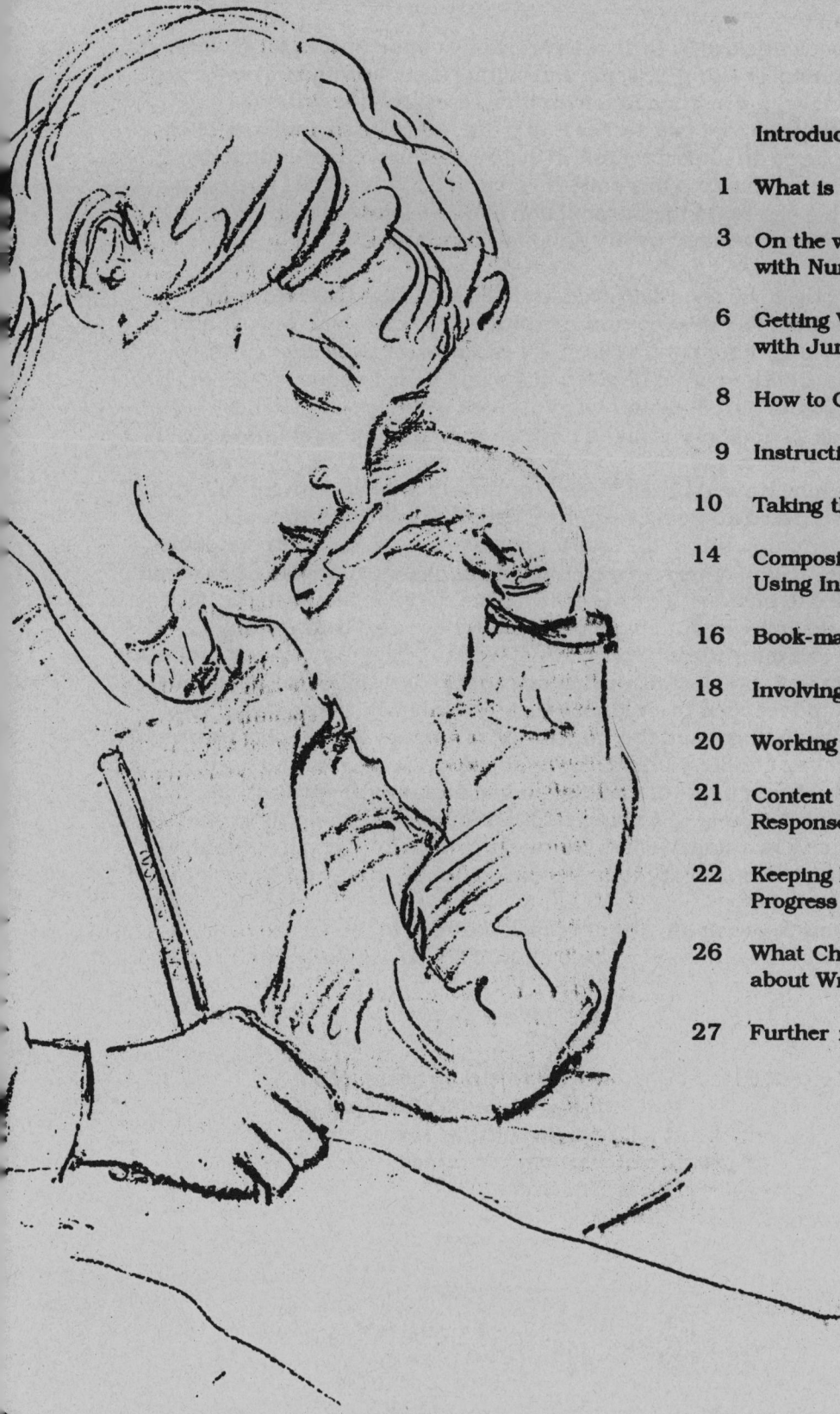

INTRODUCTION

The concerns set out in this book are largely to do with providing opportunities for children to experience the process of planning, drafting, revising and editing their writing: the crafting of a piece of work. These concerns have a history. Much exciting research into writing development has occured during the past two decades. In more recent years the work of The National Writing Project has played an important role in disseminating and extending these findings more widely. Much of this thinking has both drawn upon and informed current good practice. As a consequence, this has led to the introduction of a developmental approach to writing in the programmes of study required by the National Curriculum.

Purpose and audience have come to be regarded as central to the writing task. However, not all writing is to be carefully crafted. We must continue to provide children with opportunities for the kind of short - burst writing that might be used, for example, in planning or framing areas of enquiry and research. Children must be given many and varied opportunities to see that language is used for a range of purposes and an awareness of its appropriateness should be central to our work. The self as audience is also a dimension that must be acknowledged.

The Writers' Workshop especially, can enable children to write and publish with a real sense of audience and to receive considered audience response. With this approach they will produce fewer pieces of finished work, but in the crafting of a piece, considerable confidence will be gained in selecting and writing of text, of which the child has a true sense of ownership. Opportunities are also afforded to revisit a piece of writing, considering it afresh in the light of new experience. Through the samples of draft work collected we can also begin to build a picture of children's writing achievements and constraints. We can begin to construct profiles of their language development in a way that accurately records progression. This approach affords occasions to monitor and respond to children's early attempts at "play writing". Through the provision of writing corners and the integration of literacy in role-play we are also able to recognise what young children already know about language. We can usefully identify the strategies they use, for example, in making phonic attempts at spelling, and put this knowledge to good use. It is this kind of detailed information that will help us to plan more diagnostically for children's learning needs and make provision for the achievement of National Curriculum attainment targets at appropriate levels.

In conclusion, some of our aims in promoting the approach outlined in the following pages find recognition in the National Curriculum Proposals for English 5 - 16, June 1989:

"Good primary teachers pay attention to the process of writing, developed from knowledge and understanding of the practice of experienced writers (including themselves); they are then able to provide classroom practices which allow children to behave like real writers".

What is a Writers' Workshop?

A Writers' Workshop approach sets out to help children see themselves as real writers. Its ultimate aim is to enable children to write willingly, fluently and with confidence for a wide range of purposes and audiences. The approach draws on evidence from research into the development of writing which has been carried out over the last twenty years or so. This research views writing development not simply as a progression of skills to be acquired and practised but as a process where attention has to be paid to what is being said, to representing words in written form and to the confident use of the writing implement. Many skills are orchestrated at any one time; at any moment one skill, rather than another, will command the main part of the writer's attention.

The Writing Environment

The environment in which children write is an important aspect of this approach. Children should have access to a wide range of books of many kinds, and to objects, artefacts and activities which invite investigation and experimentation. These should reflect varied cultural and linguistic experiences. (see p16 for further ideas).

Children should be invited to draw on their own experiences in their writing. These are likely to be most readily expressed in the form of story, simple diary-entry, or poetry. The children's command of these forms will be enriched by their own encounters with them in books they have read, and in film, on radio and on television. Writers' Workshop can also provide opportunities for children to write persuasively, and to construct argument and informational pieces with particular audiences and purposes in mind.

In order to create a climate of a community of writers in the classroom it is important to make provision for quiet writing times. There will be occasions when all the children will write together; there will be others when an individual or group of children will require a quiet writing area in order to focus on their experiences. For this purpose, a corner of the classroom, designated the writing corner, has been found to be useful.

Drafting and self-editing

Part of writing development is the increasing recognition on the part of the writer of what needs to be done for the writing to accomplish its purpose. For this to happen, children need to be able to work on a piece of writing over extended periods of time. They need time for drafting and revising, time for consultation and discussion with a teacher and with other children, time for self-editing and for publishing. Access to word processing facilities can make a real difference to the child's willingness to work towards the final product, both at the redrafting and at the self-editing stage.

Publishing

Finally, publication is an important feature of the Writers' Workshop approach. Publication gives the writer access to audience. The promise of publication provides a child with an incentive to write with a clear sense of purpose, and for a specified audience.

Publication should promote the writing of children of all abilities in the following kinds of formats:

- stories
- personal stories
- message boards
- poem posters
- poetry

- letters
- scripts
- reviews
- menus
- recipes

and in the form of:

- books
- reports
- posters
- cartoon/story strips
- pamphlets
- performance
- tape and video recordings

Bookmaking

The publishing of children's texts clearly links with practical book-making activities. On pages 16 and 17 is an example of how you might begin. The emphasis on the appropriate use and quality of materials in this activity, again, provides important opportunities for the valuing of each child's work. Working links can also usefully be made with other areas of the arts and with curriculum themes and integrated subject areas embracing science, humanities and environmental studies.

ON THE WAY TO WRITERS' WORKSHOP
WITH NURSERY/INFANT CHILDREN IN MIND

Children come to statutory schooling at five with varying amounts of knowledge about the writing process. They will have seen, in real life as well as on the television, people filling in forms, writing letters, signing cheques, leaving notes, writing parking tickets. They will have handled crayons, pencils, biros, felt tips, chalk. They will have made marks on walls, in wet sand, on damp windows, in notebooks, on bits of paper. Some will have grasped the symbolic significance of marks on paper. Some will be able to write their name, some will be able to write several letters or even words; some will know something of organisation on the page.

The quality of the spoken language environment is crucial. Children's writing is greatly influenced by the amount and variety of opportunities they are given for genuine discussion, by the wealth of stories and poems their teachers share with them and by the book browsing they engage in with their friends or on their own.

The implications for the classroom are

> ∞ to listen carefully to what children say and to respond with
> interest so as to help them learn about others as language
> users and to help them realise that their own storying is valued.

> ∞ to observe children carefully so we know as much as possible
> about what and how they learn and where their real interests lie.

> ∞ to provide opportunities for children to accommodate new
> knowledge and make it their own by engaging in purposeful
> activities in meaningful contexts in all areas of the curriculum.

Ways to Show that Writing Matters

> ∞ engage in purposeful writing acts ourselves in front
> of the children.

> ∞ display writing and include it in daily discussion.

> ∞ respond warmly to all remarks young children make.

> ∞ ensure that all writing is for a real purpose and never
> a meaningless practice exercise.

Things To Do

Provide opportunities for 'real' writing to take place in role play situations such as

> ∞ telephone memo pads
> ∞ notes for the milkman
> ∞ shopping lists
> ∞ price tags
> ∞ sale notices
> ∞ receipts
> ∞ cheques
> ∞ order forms
> ∞ tickets for trains, buses,
> planes, cinema, theatre

> ∞ labels
> ∞ posters
> ∞ programmes
> ∞ menus
> ∞ bills
> ∞ signposts
> ∞ charts
> ∞ passports

The following activities have also been found to be very supportive in encouraging early writing:

Writers' Corner

All authors have different preferences in terms of environment and implements. This is also true for children. It is therefore important to provide in a quiet area:

⁍ a variety of paper of different sizes, shapes,
colours and textures, lined, unlined, headed,
some suitable for scroll making.

⁍ a variety of writing implements such as pencils
(thin and thick), coloured pencils, biros,
coloured felt tips, (thin & thick), writing
brushes and ink stones, chalks, quills, reed
pens, stylus.

⁍ envelopes. Start saving used ones for this purpose.
This could also be a first step in introducing the use
of recycled paper with young children

⁍ staplers and sellotape, occasionally, if available.

Observe individual children's reactions at the writing corner. Some may simply take pleasure from the sensory experience of drawing pen across paper; some may list known letters or figures, some may set out to convey a message. Accept and value whatever a child offers and take your cue from that in terms of the response you make.

Message Board

A message board provides an opportunity for dialogue in writing and reinforces the notion that writing has meaning for adults other than teachers.

•• set up a message board in a prominent place where
visitors, parents, teachers and children from
all classes can leave messages for each other.

Interactive Displays

Interactive displays provide opportunities for children to write for a purpose, in response to written questions posed by the teacher or by peers in relation to the topic theme.

Therefore,

•• provide enough space and implements for children
to respond in writing

•• perhaps provide a reply box

Message Books

These allow for written responses which indirectly provide a model for children of fluent written language use.

•• give an individual message book or journal to
each child

➥ either write special messages overnight for the
  children to discover in the morning or write
  whenever a particular child wants to start or
  continue a dialogue with you

➥ respect authors' privacy should they prefer to
  write a private message to a friend on occasion

Sharing the Writing

Once you have engendered enthusiasm for writing, it is important that you continue to focus children's attention on writing activities and devote a short time each day, if possible, to sharing children's writing as a group.

"Let's see if there are any letters in our post box today."
"Is that a new message on our board?"
"Don't forget to take your special note home for grandma, **Waseef**."

Supporting Early Writers

➥ aim for a balance between teacher-guided and
  child-initiated writing

➥ with teacher-guided writing always ensure that
  the children see the relevance of the activity
  and are clear about the intended audience

➥ it is valuable to allow children to co-operate
  sometimes to produce a joint story or book
  (this is especially valuable for a child who
  needs support for a short period of time).

We feel we cannot be prescriptive about age-related achievements since children develop at such different rates. However, try to have the following observations in mind; this should help you to support young children in their writing.

➥ initially content will be egocentric.
  Immediacy is usual for young children rather
  than reflection.

➥ rehearsing in another medium, e.g. drawings,
  talking, painting, model making, is common.

➥ cohesion factors may well be limited to "and"
  "then" "so".

➥ retelling well-loved stories is a natural
  part of the developmental process
  and provides an opportunity for
  children to reconstruct a
  narrative and make it
  their own.

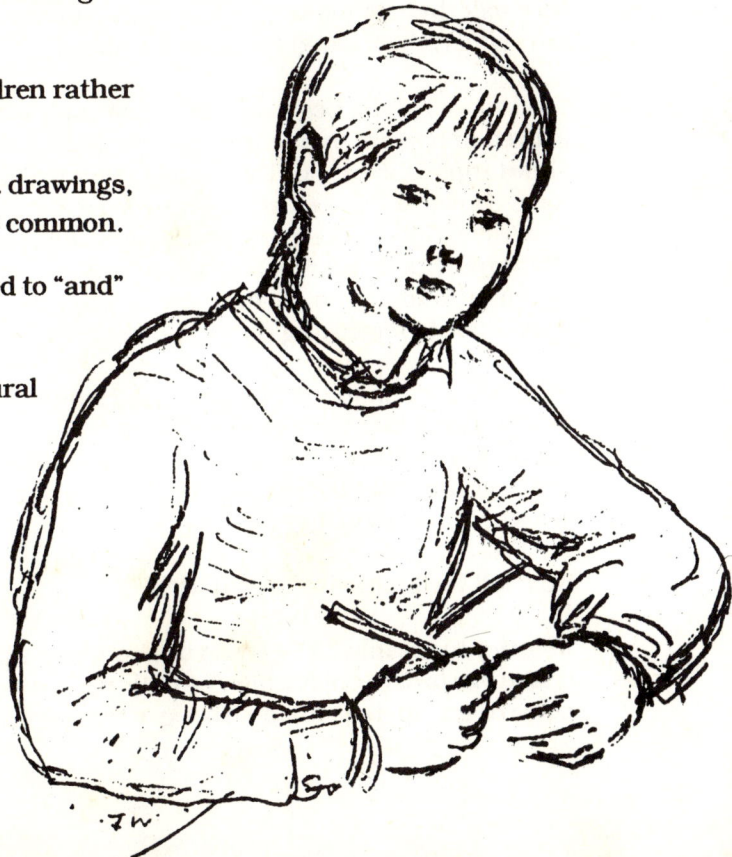

GETTING WRITERS' WORKSHOP STARTED WITH JUNIOR CHILDREN IN MIND

For children to feel confident to experiment at a later stage, they must initially feel secure in the expectations made of them. For this reason it is important to follow a careful procedure which quickly becomes familiar to the children. For children to see writing as a process the teacher must write with them, demonstrating how she selects topic, gets started, proceeds, is hindered, sometimes struggles still with writing. Thus it is possible to make explicit to children the strategies and techniques adopted by a mature writer, and through discussion help them to incorporate these approaches actively in their work.

1. Write down on a good-sized piece of paper or OHP transparency 3 or 4 topics to write about which are of immediate interest to you and that you think will interest the children, e.g.

   a. Where we used to live: what my family remembers.
   b. The new kittens.
   c. The day I met Bernard Ashley.
   d. What you can see in Sulham Woods.

   While doing this, talk to the children about how you chose the topics. Help them to see that often a writer struggles with topic choice.

2. Now, select one of your topics and explain to the children why you have chosen this one to write about. Tell them something about why you have rejected the others for now.

3. Give the children sheets of paper and ask them to write down two topics they think will be interesting to write about.

4. A few minutes later, ask the children to write down two more topics

5. Now ask them to make the choice of a topic out of the four which they would like to write about.

6. Your model at the beginning of the session will have proved important in helping children to feel confident about topic choice. For this session you will probably have chosen a topic close to your own experience. You can invite the children, implicitly or explicitly, to do the same, but if you find that some children have still not made a topic choice, then you might invite them to write about 'Something that happened yesterday/today'.

7. Tell the children to turn to their neighbour, and taking only 2 minutes each, explain why they have chosen that particular topic to write about. In this activity lies the beginning of the response partner work that you will develop further at a later stage.

8. Now tell the children to begin writing.

9. In order to establish the sense of a community of writers it is important to encourage the children, whether whole class or group, to focus on the experience by writing in silence.

Write with the Children

1. As the children begin to write, the teacher does also, for about 5-6 minutes.

2. After this period of time walk round.

Sharing the work

1. After about 15-20 minutes writing, and no longer on the first session, bring the children together in a circle to talk about their experiences.

   Some of the areas to talk about might be:

   ∞ what were some of the topics?

   ∞ what did it feel like to be writing like this?
   Perhaps here the teacher might share some of her experiences, including any difficulties she had

   ∞ and then, an invitation to the children to read some of what they have written so far - this might only be a sentence. At this stage it would be appropriate to share only three or four pieces of writing and to listen carefully and then respond to the <u>content</u> of the work. It is important, also, to provide opportunities for the children to ask questions of the writers

2. Tell the children when the next Writers' Workshop sessions will be and that you and they will be writing together again on these occasions.

3. Make a list of the names of the children who you now recognise need help. During succeeding sessions spend a little time with them at regular intervals.

These are guidelines for establishing Writers' Workshop. Later you will develop your own approaches and practices which best work for you and the particular children with whom you work.

HOW TO ORGANISE A WRITERS' WORKSHOP

To set up a Writers' Workshop corner in your classroom, you will need:

- ❧ a manilla folder for each child, or a book, depending on the individual's writing preferences

- ❧ a cardboard box, divided alphabetically, for storing folders

- ❧ a box for completed work awaiting binding and publication

- ❧ paper of different standard sizes (A4, B3, A6) both lined and unlined, for drafting

- ❧ paper for publishing

- ❧ access to a typewriter or a word-processor

- ❧ thick card for making book covers cut to sizes according to paper size

- ❧ plenty of sharpened pencils

- ❧ a variety of pens, including coloured felt tips and calligraphic pens and other specialist writing implements

- ❧ a rota of children with responsibility for checking pencils, pens and paper

- ❧ a sign-up sheet for children awaiting consultation

- ❧ a set of records for recording each child's progress (see Keeping Records p.18)

INSTRUCTIONS TO CHILDREN

Effective organisation is instrumental in ensuring that Writers' Workshop activities are a success. Essential to this is providing very clear instructions to the children that provide a clear structure in which to work.

"We will be aiming to have your writing published and made into books for everyone to enjoy."

"When I am writing I do not want interruptions!"

"Neither do we!"

"When I am talking to a child about her writing I do not want to be interrupted."

"If you want more paper or a sharpened pencil during the lesson you must help yourself."

"If you don't have a topic, don't panic, I'll come and talk with you."

"You will be asked to write down two topics of interest to you."

"If you think of any new topics to write about, add the title to the list on the inside of your folder under 'New Ideas to Write About'."

"The FOLDER goes in the box behind the letter of your name."

"ALL your writing - including rough notes & drafts is to be kept in your folder."

"You will be asked to write down two more topics of interest to you."

"We will be doing this kind of writing again to-morrow."

"I will see you during your writing time - wait until I come to see you."

"You will then be given some time to talk to your neighbour about why you think that topic would be good to write about."

"You will then be asked to choose one topic to write about from your four titles."

TAKING THE WRITING FURTHER

For children to become fluent, autonomous writers, it is vital to respond to every writing attempt with genuine interest. Writing alongside children is a particularly positive support, as is the use of tapes, typewriters and word-processors. Talk about publishing is invaluable and perhaps might include the opportunity to look at an author's proofs of familiar books. Links should be made continuously between the child as reader and as writer; the one feeding the experience of the other.

For Early Writers

- right from the start, encourage children to share their writing with the rest of the class. Storytime is an ideal opportunity and puts children on a par with 'real' authors.

- take every opportunity to extend the audience: other teachers, the Head, parents, dinner supervisors, caretakers, secretaries, the whole school in assembly. All enjoy hearing children's stories when given the opportunity.

- make your main focus the children composing and developing their own authorial voice.

- always write a comment on the **content**. We see this as crucial for the writer to know that she has written something of interest and to know the teacher is an interested reader.

- think carefully about using the happy face symbol as a response. It is, of course, a warm, friendly gesture but it does not provide a further writing model for the child, nor does it afford an opportunity to continue the dialogue between reader and writer.

- handwriting skills take time to develop so be prepared to help out if a child tires. Typewriters and word-processors are most useful here too.

- try out a class wordbook rather than individual ones. This encourages children to take a mental picture of a word and commit it to memory.

- while on the way to becoming a reflective writer, a child will need help, in an individual consultation, to organise material, to decide where to start, to group relevant comments together etc. Suggest arrows, or a numbering system for cutting and pasting. Children become independent by working in pairs and then small group conferences.

- at this stage do not insist on redrafting. Not every piece of writing will need it, and not every child can cope with it yet.

- do not insist on a fair copy. Adults can act as 'publishers', if necessary, and produce the finished product which the child could feel pleased with.

- leave editing till last. Praise near misses and sensible analogies in spelling. Then, from these choose 1 or 2 specific items, and no more at this stage, to discuss.

Suggestions for Nursery and Infant Children

- ☞ try to set up a 'publishing' firm and 'publish' books of children's work such as a collection of class stories, an anthology of stories from different children, a book of favourite poems, a picture book, recipe books, sets of instructions.

- ☞ photos, children's drawings and paintings, postcards, newspaper cuttings can be used to illustrate the books. Children will also enjoy choosing wrapping paper or designing covers, as well as drawing decorative borders for the pages. Think of making use of recurring letter patterns to help develop fluent letter forms and spatial awareness.

- ☞ set up an 'Author(s) of The Week' board to highlight the writings of either an established author or particular child or children in the class, perhaps, with a photo or self-portrait and biographical details.

Writers' Workshop Consultations

The early discussions about a child's piece of writing might be with another child or with the teacher. The emphasis will be on the meaning conveyed, with talk about form and sequence of events and suitability for the intended audience. Very helpful at this stage, both to the children involved and in terms of effective classroom organisation, is for children to work as response partners. They will take turns to listen to and look at each other's work, agreeing that there will be no interruptions whilst they speak.

With children new to this approach it is helpful to suggest that their first response to a child's work should be a positive one:-

- ● what did they like about it?

- ● is there anything else that might be included?

- ● next, they might discuss - Are there any parts that don't sound right?

- ● Is it suitable for the person or people who will read it?
  For example, a younger child or an older person?

- ● does anything need to be changed for this particular audience?

When children work together in this way they are helped towards critically using and shaping the language.

Work in progress or ready for publication may need to be discussed at length. You will need to plan for this. Children will have been reminded that the first draft is not necessarily a rough copy which will be written out neatly and that they can make as many rough drafts and alterations as they need to. To help them concentrate on content and form at the earlier stages, and to prepare for the consultations, the children should be asked to use the following self-editing devices in preparation for the discussion:

    〰️ under sections of the text that do not 'sound right' and require further thought and discussion

    ▢ around punctuation points to be discussed

    ◯ to mark spellings they are unsure about

The child might have worked on this proof-reading with a response partner prior to the consultation with the teacher.

Consultations will be needed when children have:

➨ reached a certain stage in the writing and feel that they need to discuss it

➨ completed a piece of writing and need to talk about it, perhaps prior to publishing

Classroom organisation

➨ it is helpful to ask children who require consultations to put their work in a box marked CONSULTATIONS and to sign their names on a sign-up sheet. This will provide you with a ready record of the children who are bringing work forward in any one week. It also provides the opportunity to plan either for pupil response partner work at this stage, or for consultations with the teacher or other supporting adults.

➨ during any one session ensure that you organise for a number of consultations. When involved in these yourself, always sit next to or near the child.

During the Consultation

➨ allow the child time to think and talk at his/her own pace

➨ ask enabling and extending questions and try to avoid being too prescriptive

➨ use some of the vocabulary of the writing process in your discussions - revising, redrafting, publication

➨ talk about adding to or altering the piece

➨ change the spelling discussed. Ask the children to write the conventional ones in their own dictionaries

➨ together discuss and correct punctuation

➨ in the process of editing and revising, help the children to take the role of reader

➨ ask again about suitability for intended audience and give your own views

➨ talk about whether the intended meaning is fully conveyed

➨ discuss 'how it reads'.

Keep a Record

♦ make a note in your record file of any points
    discussed. Note achievements and difficulties.
    (see section on Keeping Records of Children's Progress, p.18)

Group Conferences

♦ from keeping a close record of children's work
    you will notice those who are experiencing
    similar difficulties at a particular time, for
    example with the use of quotation marks.
    Bring these children together and work as a
    group, in this case reading aloud and discussing
    where the quotation marks should be placed.

Publishing gives a great sense of achievement in being an author. Not all pieces will be
published and it is usual for the teacher and child to decide on this together. After the first
piece of work, perhaps about one in five will be published. In relation to publication you
need to consider:

♦ production of the text - will it be handwritten
    - in ink or pencil, jumbo or ordinary typeface,
    or word-processed?

♦ the cover, and how the book will be made.
    What type of illustrations will be used?
    How will they sit with the text?

♦ the size and shape of the publication.
    At various times children find it equally engaging
    to produce very small, large or unusually shaped
    books.

♦ the use of photographs

♦ a biography of the author

♦ a contents page and summary, if relevant

♦ a dual-text publication

♦ translations and transliterations
    of other languages

At this stage it is important to draw
upon community involvement,
where possible.

COMPOSING AND PUBLISHING : USING INFORMATION TECHNOLOGY

Using Information Technology - computers and different types of printers can help with the process of writing, and with publishing:

- ❖ it is simple to produce successive drafts by altering an existing one,

- ❖ it enables experiments with different sequences and ordering of a text,

- ❖ it makes editing and proof-reading easier,

- ❖ it offers particularly appropriate opportunities for collaborative work, especially for parent helpers working with children,

- ❖ it can boost the self-esteem of children who are not confident writers, or who have specific learning difficulties with writing,

- ❖ it can help children achieve levels of presentation in publishing their work, including the use of sophisticated layout and different typefaces as made avilable in desktop publishing,

- ❖ with desktop publishing, a much wider range of real audiences is opened up. Children can produce books which really do look like real books, and a wide variety of printed communications to a high standard.

Getting started

The minimum equipment you need to use IT as part of Writers' Workshop is:

- ☞ a computer equipped with a disk drive or hard disk, and a good supply of disks,
- ☞ simple word-processing software such as Prompt Writer (MESU) and Write,
- ☞ A printer which your software recognises for printing in different sizes and styles.

Make the IT facilities an attractive part of the Workshop environment.

Most writers find it easiest to print out a draft, then mark up corrections by hand before returning to redraft. Use clear symbols which show where text will be moved—this will help give the children a sense of the way facilities can be used. If you have friends or know writers who use word-processing for writing that might interest the children, try collecting samples of their edited drafts and final versions.

Think about keeping successive drafts and final versions to show to the children, and use them to introduce word processing as part of the Workshop.

Using word processing in the Writers' Workshop

All children need to have access to word-processing facilities in the course of a school year. In deciding which children have access at which time, it may be helpful to bear in mind the following:

- ❖ many children who are otherwise reluctant writers may be strongly motivated by the opportunity to produce printed texts,
- ❖ children who have specific handwriting or spelling difficulties can find it encouraging to use word-processing facilities,

◆ a collaborative writing task involving the production of very short texts (captions, working comments etc.) is likely to enable many children to gain experience in a short period of time. Writing tasks like these are particulary appropriate for classes just beginning computer use,

◆ involving adults as (computer) scribes for pupils may aviod the problem of unfamiliarity with keyboards which can slow down children's first efforts.

Working with emergent writers

Just as we have learnt to encourage forms of emergent writing produced with pencils and pens, we need also to recognise the "playing with the keyboard" may be another form of emergent writing. See what happens if you offer children opportunities to save print-out and talk about what they have typed.

Some more advanced features

with word processing software that provides:
- Very attractive screen displays
- A wide variety of typefaces (e.g. FOLIO and PENDOWN).
- The facility to produce non-Roman alphabets with the use of special Keyboard and overlay (FOLIO for the BBC and ALLWRITE for the RM Nimbus).
- Extra features to help with editing, e.g. a dictionary facility and outliner for early drafts (PENDOWN).

Towards real print

As the essence of Writer's Workshop is producing "real writing" for real audiences, the prospect of producing "real print" is very exciting. In order to do this it is necessary to have access to a laser printer as well as a powerful computer and DTP software. Laser printers are very costly and may seem beyond primary schools. However, Teachers' Centres and LEA computer centres are increasingly being equipped with all facilities needed. One solution is for a teacher or parent perhaps working with a small group of children, to go to a centre where they can work on the layout and print-out of texts they have drafted in the classroom. Because secondary schools are increasingly being equipped with DTP facilities, this could offer a focus for a cross-phase collaborative writing project.

Where it is possible to offer children laser printer output, it is well worth devoting time to developing the children's print/graphic awareness:

◆ display and encourage the children to bring in samples of print in different typestyles and sizes

◆ display printers' charts and handbooks showing different typefaces and the uses made of them

◆ try to collect or borrow old sample printers' blocks and letters (avoid lead or other potentially harmful materials).

Make discussion of print-out choices part of Conferences:

◆ when sharing books with children, draw attention to the way in which they have been designed

◆ invite a practising typographer or designer to show her/his work.

BOOK-MAKING

BOOK MAKING ACTIVITY

HERE IS AN EXAMPLE OF BOOK-MAKING WHICH CAN BE EASILY MODIFIED TO MAKE BOOKS OF DIFFERENT SIZES AND SHAPES:

To make a small notebook, that could be used as a journal, diary, or for publishing children's individual stories as an outcome of Writers' Workshop activities, you will need:

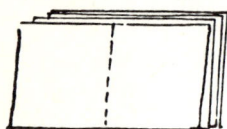

5 - 8 sheets of A4 typing paper, folded in half, for pages.

1 sheet, again A4 size, of coloured sugar paper, quality paper or thin card for the end papers.

1 strip of strong paper, selotape cloth or book binding tape for the spine, 5 cm. wide and 6 cm longer than the long sides of the book pages. The same paper as the end papers can be used as long as it is strong enough.

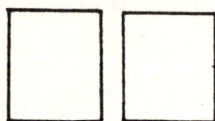

2 stiff pieces of cardboard for the covers. Each one needs to be the same size as the pages when folded in half. The cardboard back of a pad of A4 file paper is extremely suitable; it simply needs cutting in half with a sharp cutting tool!

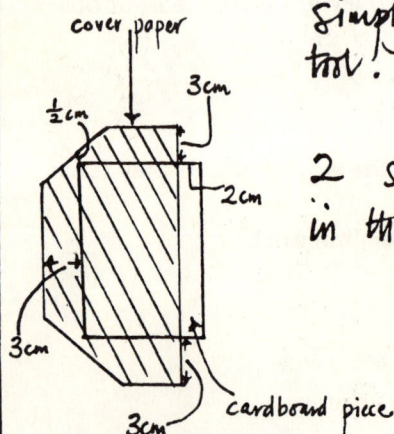

2 sheets of covering paper, cut as shown in this diagram.

cover paper

3cm

½cm

2cm

3cm

3cm

cardboard piece

METHOD

1. Fold pages and end papers in half with a sharp crease and sew together as follows:

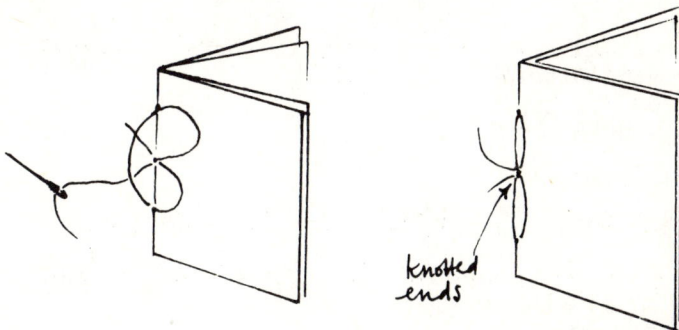

knotted ends

2. Paste spine to boards as shown below. Fold the spine over to the inside and paste.

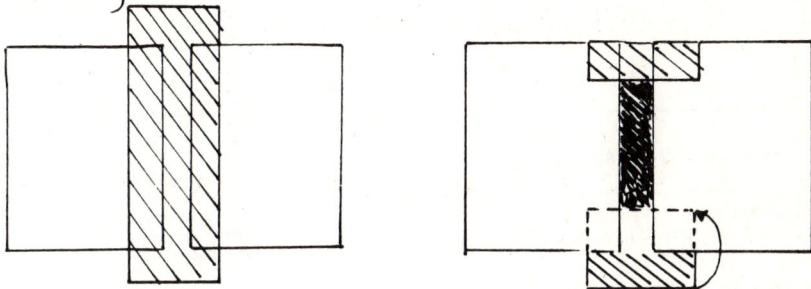

3. Paste covers to boards

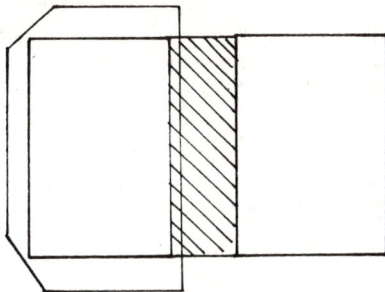

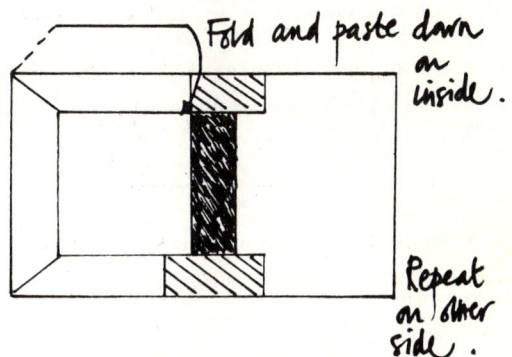

Fold and paste down on inside.

Repeat on other side.

4.

Cover

pages of book with end paper on top

Put book pages in position. Paste end papers to inside cover, first on one side, then on the other.

INVOLVING PARENTS AND THE COMMUNITY

Together teachers, parents, and other carers of children can make a unique contribution. It is important to reassure parents that one of the best things they can do is let their children see them writing and giving it meaning. Equally, that they should respond positively to their children's writing. They can also encourage the child to feel part of a 'writing family'. Encouraging a child to reciprocate, or indeed initiate communications with aunts, uncles, grandparents is an enjoyable way of doing this.

This is real news!
Grandpa has been given a bee hive (humming with bees!) and the Jennings down the lane are looking after a donkey. When can you come and see? much love, Grandma.

James Goodwin,
4, Church Street,
BRISTOL
B8X 4R1.

Here is an example of how one school communicated with its parents in order to provide them with information about the Writers' Workshop approach and how they might help:

Writers' Workshop

What is Writers' Workshop?

- All the children have their own folder. On the front page there is a list of stories which they have written, on the inside cover there is a list of ideas for stories and on the next page a list of their skills (for instance, full stops and capital letters, quotation marks...).

- First children choose their subject and do a *rough draft* of their story.

- When they have finished they *self-edit* the story, using the following symbols

  ⁓ when they think they have wrongly spelled a word

  ☐ when they think they have missed out a full stop

  ⌇ when something just doesn't make sense

- Next they ask for a *consultation* with the teacher or another adult. The teacher then works through the story with them, providing any spelling they need, making suggestions for ways of extending the story, etc.

- Finally, the children *publish* the story, writing it out in neat and illustrating it.

Why is Writers' Workshop a good idea?

- It helps children to understand that writing is a process, and that you have to work at it to get good results.

- Because the technical aspects of writing - good spelling and neat handwriting - are left until later the children are free to get on with the business of composing a good story. They tend to write at much greater length and really enjoy what they are doing.

- Because their work is published and circulated, they are writing for a real audience and not just hiding their efforts in an exercise book. This gives their writing a much greater sense of purpose. Self-editing is a very useful skill which it is good to develop from the earliest possible time.

How to help a child doing writers' Workshop

- Check that the child has self-edited.

- Start the consultation by talking about the subject of the story. Then get the child to read the story to you.

- Praise the child when you reach a point where they have self-edited.

- If they have spelled a word wrongly, praise them for making a good attempt and provide the correct spelling above, in the margin, at the bottom of the page or on a separate sheet, depending on how they have set the story out.

- If the story is bland or doesn't make sense, ask questions which will help them think of expanding the story or making it clear. Help them to write any additions to the story.

- At the end provide lots more praise and write a comment which shows you've really enjoyed reading the strory.

Supporting Parent Helpers

It is important to provide support for any helpers involved. Make sure everyone fully understands how the organisation of the approach works, by full briefing meetings, or a hand-out, pamphlet or a video.

It is equally important to respect adults' preferences, for instance, about working inside or outside the classroom, with their own child or not, with an individual or small group.

The following activities have all been undertaken successfully by adult helpers:

- typing children's finished work to go on display or into a book

- transferring finished work onto a word processor with printer

- assembling a finished book

- consultations to discuss organisation, redrafting, omissions, additions

- final editing of surface features such as spelling, punctuation

- co-operative writing activities with a small group

- co-operative writing activity with a child as partner,
  e.g. writing a book together for a younger child

- translating children's English texts into community languages

- writing down traditional stories from community cultures

WORKING WITH BILINGUAL PUPILS

When working with a bilingual or emerging bilingual child using English as a second language, it is important to keep at the forefront of our concerns the need for the child to experience in writing the flow and fluency of sustained narrative.

For this reason it may well be appropriate to make available the opportunity for the child to do some writing in the first language, if literate in both. Here, parental and possibly community help will need to be sought. To use an example, you may invite the parent of a Japanese speaking child into school to talk about the possibility of the child writing some stories in Japanese. These would be shared in school and, as importantly, with the family at home. In this way the child is still able to experience writing continuous, cohesive text, whilst at the early stages of learning English.

In other circumstances it may be appropriate to arrange for the text resulting from Writers' Workshop activities to be produced in dual-text editions, or parallel texts, separately published. If a language of Asian or other origin is used, together with English, then a transliteration of the Asian origin text will enable access to the pronounciation of that language to all members of the class. This is an opportunity that can provide very positive openings for acknowledging language diversity. In achieving this, we may draw on the services of the relevant support agencies for language and intercultural work, and where possible, invite the involvement of parents and other community members.

The following are important activities applicable to <u>all classrooms</u>, which can help to establish an atmosphere supportive of linguistic diversity:-

- provide alphabet charts in a range of languages. These might include Punjabi, Arabic, Hindi, Urdu, Russian, Greek, Hebrew alongside the Roman script

- Numerals to 10 in a range of languages

- a 'newspaper rack' in the home corner, class or school library where newspapers in Bengali, Welsh, Urdu, German, French, Turkish could find a place

- intersperse the rhymes and action songs children learn so readily with some in different languages and dialects and translated from a variety of cultures

- ensure that the images displayed in school and classroom show the range of cultures in Britain today and help to lead outward to a wider world perspective

- part of the regular reading diet offered to children will be a range of folk tales, poems and stories from around the world

- include in the book stock of the school, books written in community languages, dual-text publications, and taped stories in a range of languages

- provide a variety of writing implements

- encourage members of the community to become involved with the children in practical writing activities, including working on translations and transliterations of text

CONTENT THAT CAUSES CONCERN: RESPONSE AND INTERVENTION

In the Writers' Workshop approach children are invited to make independent topic choices. This close involvement ensures a greater engagement with the writing experience and increased motivation to work at the craft of writing. The valuing of a child's work through publishing adds also to the sense of enjoyment and ownership that can be experienced.

Once released from the constraints of teacher imposed topics, children may on occasion produce writing of a kind that causes the teacher concern. The concern may derive from limited and repetitive use of genre (the stereotypical space fantasy for instance) and of stylistic devices. This concern may include children repeatedly using violent imagery in their writing. The response of the teacher is critical here. Where the child's models for writing are clearly limited they need to be fed by introducing a richer variety of narrative models. Explicit discussion between the teacher and pupils as a group or whole class about limited and stereotypic writing models would also be an important response. Sensitivity of response is essential to the developing confidence of a young author but this must allow for the teacher to respond with honesty and integrity to the content of a child's work.

Clearly, then, it is not just the quality of support that ensures success with this approach. It is also the quality of teacher intervention and of a classroom environment in which considerable knowledge about books is drawn on and in which ideas and influences - particularly those from the media - are critically discussed.

To help practically, here are some suggestions:

What might you do if ....?

A child disparages members of other cultures

- Don't ignore it.
  Address what the child has written in a conference.

- Tell the child why you and others in the school find
  what is written offensive. Help the child to develop
  a sense of readership and to see that a reader whom
  this might concern would be distressed by the content.

- Where appropriate invoke codes of playground and
  school behaviour which are concerned with making
  respectful relationships.

A child writes in a confiding way to the teacher, but signalling outside school experiences which may give cause for concern
(for instance an indication of sexual abuse)

- Recognise that it is important to respond but don't
  feel that you should do this alone.

- Involve other professionals in the school, including your
  Headteacher, and seek support from them about making
  a further response.

- You will be anxious about breaching the child's confidence
  in you. Remember that any child will want to have the
  distress they experience acknowledged in the hope that
  there might be a resolution. If this is recognised, then
  it is with the child's agreement that the experience, first
  written about privately, is shared with others.

KEEPING RECORDS OF CHILDREN'S PROGRESS WITH WRITERS' WORKSHOP

You will need to keep a weekly check on what progress your children are making with their writing.

Organise it like this:

> •• divide the class into five groups
> (e.g. class of 30 children x 5 = 6 children per group)

> •• post a list of each group in your Writers'
> Workshop corner

MONDAY GROUP	TUESDAY GROUP	WEDNESDAY GROUP	THURSDAY GROUP	FRIDAY GROUP
Helen Tracy Lisa	Robert Leroy David	Amanda Alif Paul	Jonathan Manjit Sophie	

> •• collect the folders from the Monday group each Monday

> •• take the folders away for diagnosis of difficulty and
> recording of progress

> •• return folders on the following day and have a brief
> consultation with each child

> •• where a child is obviously stuck, or needs more attention,
> make time for a personal consultation during the next
> writing session

Form of Record

You will need to keep a record of your weekly check on what progress your children are making with their writing. This should take the form of a child record and a teacher record.

The Child Record

The child record should be kept on the inside back cover of the folder. It should be a list of the child's achievements. Add to it as necessary.

Writing skills Jane can use:
- Build-up of story to climax.
- Use of aside to reader.
- Writing story as a play.
- Proof-reading for spelling mistakes.
- Capital letter at start of writing.
- Full stop at end of sentence.

The Teacher Record

The purpose of the teacher record is to help you recognise the child's achievements in writing and possible current constraints.

You will need a loose-leaved file, or a card index, alphabetically ordered with each child's name

NAME: _____		
Date	Progress	Error — diagnosis
19/1/88	Consistently correct spelling of 'said' (instead of 'siad' as used previously).	Events of narrative in confused sequence.
26/1/88	Hand - writing less uneven.	Poor sense of audience in evidence.
2/2/88	Events of narrative well sequenced.	Some use of commas instead of full - stops.
9/2/88	Use of aside to the reader	Muddled over use of apostrophes.

Alternatively (or in addition), prepare a class set of guidelines for monitoring writing progress (see over).

For the class teacher, keeping a longitudinal record of a child's progress from term to term and year to year is very helpful. Examples of work can be interleaved with record sheets.

QUESTIONS TO ASK ABOUT A PIECE OF WRITING
a sampling record (based on Irene Farmer's 'Staging Points')
This record can be used to check on progress in writing over a term or a year. You may need to allow for some uneven development.

AT level (writing)	**Achievements**												
3:1	Does the child's writing have something to tell?												
3:2	Are events set out in a logical sequence?												
3:2	Is the child beginning to indicate character, other than the self?												
	Is there an indication of feeling? *												
3:3	Does the child show awareness of audience?												
3:3	Does the child shape the story, building up to a climax?												
3:3	Do sentences have more than one clause?												
3:4	Does the child use commas appropriately?												
	Does the child attempt to use detail, or dramatise?												
3:5	Does the child use asides, or brackets?												
3:5	Does the child use repetition for effect?												
3:5	Does the child play on the meaning of words?												
AT level (writing)	**Constraints**												
<3:2	Does the child need help in getting it down on paper?												
<3:2	Does the child have difficulty in reading back what she/he has written?												
<3:3	Does the child use capital letters incorrectly?												
<3:3	Does the child omit full stops?												
<3:4	Does the tense change incorrectly?												
<3:4	Does the child repeat nouns instead of using pronouns?												
<3:4	Does the child put in full-stops unnecessarily?												
<3:4	Does the child omit commas?												
<3:4	Does the child use speech marks incorrectly?												
<3:4	Does the child have difficulty with paragraphs?												
<3:5	Does the child only use simple verbs (e.g. said, did, went?)												
<4:2	Does the child show signs of difficulty with visual retention and	a) spell common sight words phonetically?												
		b) write reversals?												

Notes:

< Indicates not yet at this level

* this operates at all levels

'The best writing is vigorous, committed, honest and interesting. We have not included these qualities in our attainment targets as they cannot be mapped on to levels. (Even so, all good practice will be geared to encouraging and fostering these vital qualities)'
Cox report para 10.19

FOLDERS.......some ideas

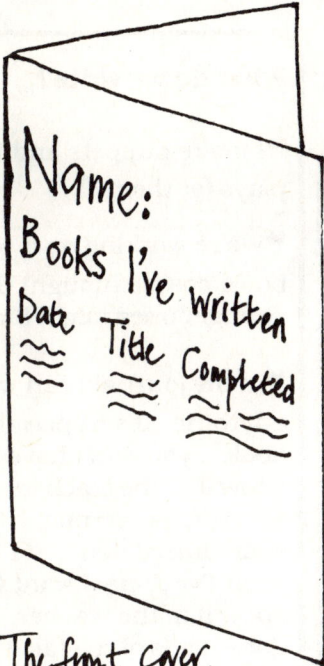

Name:
Books I've written

Date   Title   Completed

The front cover.

Sign – Up	Sheet
Day	Names
Monday	Abdul Shaffi. Sophie Law Tom Drinkwater
Tuesday	
Wednesday	
Thursday	
Friday	

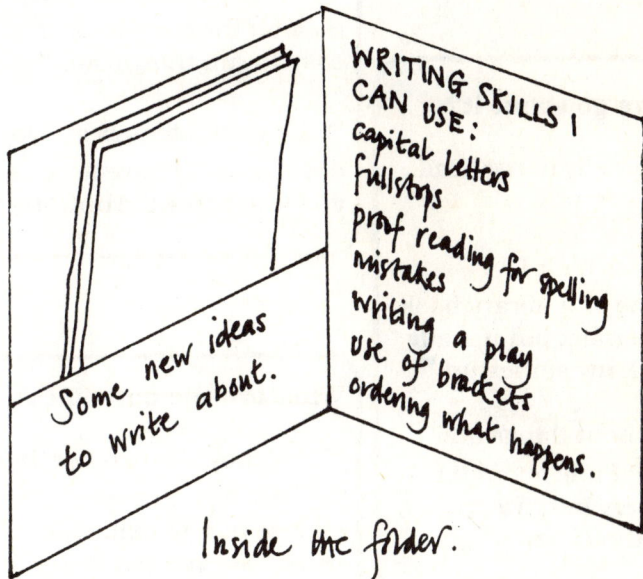

WRITING SKILLS I CAN USE:
capital letters
fullstops
proof reading for spelling mistakes
writing a play
use of brackets
ordering what happens.

Some new ideas to write about.

Inside the folder.

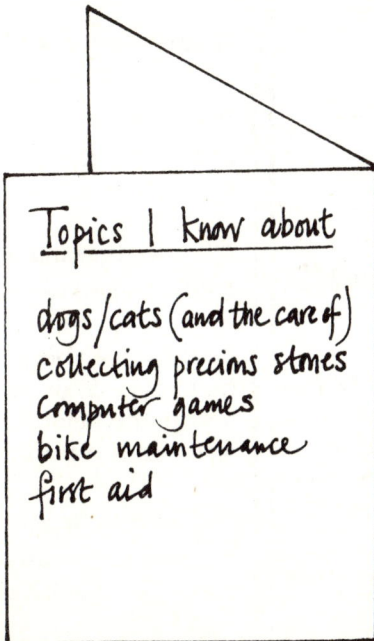

Topics I know about

dogs/cats (and the care of)
collecting precious stones
computer games
bike maintenance
first aid

The back cover.

WHAT CHILDREN HAVE TO SAY ABOUT WRITING

Why do we write?

"I like writing 'cos I can use my favourite pens... I've got a whole bag full of different coloured magic wand pens"

"I brought my friend a writing set back from Ireland 'cos I know she loves writing"

How do we go about it?

"I think quietly in my head then I do it."

"Sometimes it's a T.V. programme or a library book that I remember but usually I just think my stories up."

"I think about things and sometimes I talk about it to my very, very best friend, Kate and then I write."

What strategies do we use?

"Sometimes I change my mind and I just put a line through it."

"Sometimes I talk to Carla. If we're not quite sure, we interrupt and we tell each other and we don't lose our tempers."

"I think if my friend's got the spelling or I have a little think then I remember after a bit for myself."

What do we write with?

"I like writing in pencil best because if you do a mistake you can just rub it out."

"I like writing with pens then you don't have to rub out, just scribble it through. Pens are grown-up."

"If we're writing together, we do it on the computer - it's easy to rub things out."

"The computer's best - you don't actually have to write, you just press the buttons."

What are the outcomes?

"You show the teacher then you get it photocopied. You choose how to make the book then you put it in the book boxes for everybody to read."

"I like to have my books, photocopied so I can have one at home and one at school then all the people here can read it and I can read it but there's still a book for my family as well."

"I like to take my stories home for mum to read. She usually comments whether she likes them or not. She likes happy endings best so I can't put bad bits in them."

What do we write?

"I make puppets and I write plays for them."

"We're working on a pop-up book 'cos we thought the younger ones might like it."

"In my journal I can write anything. It's a special book... you don't have to show it to the teacher. sometimes I do and sometimes I don't. If I like what I've done, I want to show it to the teacher. If I've done loads of mistakes, I don't show it to her."

"At home, I write letters mainly to my friends ... and I write postcards to them when I'm on holiday."

"Me and Tanroy are writing a book for Nabiela."

Where do we write?

"I like writing at home and at the weekend. I do joined-up writing at home."

"I've written in my car before, when we went a long way. In the winter, we're going somewhere hot and I haven't been on an aeroplane before ... I can write on the aeroplane!"

"I like it to be quiet when I'm writing because we can't concentrate if it's not."

RECOMMENDED FOR FURTHER READING

The Writers' Workshop approach was developed by Donald Graves;
his book is therefore strongly recommended.

GRAVES, Donald   Writing: Teachers & Children at Work   Heinemann (1983)

Other recommended reading is as follows:

ATKINSON, Dorothy (ed) The Children's Bookroom, reading and the use   Trentham Books (1989)
                        of books

BARRS, Myra *et al.*   The Primary Language Record:
                        a handbook for teachers   Chameleon Press (1988)
                        available from the ILEA Centre for Language in Primary Education

BEARD, Roger   Children's Writing in the Primary School   Hodder & Stoughton (1984)

DEPARTMENT OF   English National Curriculum 5-11   HMSO (1988)
EDUCATION &   available from: National Curriculum Council, Room 608, Newcombe
SCIENCE   House, 45 Notting Hill Gate, London W11 3JB

DEPARTMENT OF   Report of the Committee of Inquiry into the
EDUCATION &   Teaching of the English Language (The Kingman Report)   HMSO (1988)
SCIENCE

FARMER, I   A Policy for Writers 9-12
                        Staging Points in Personal Narrative 1983
                        available from Language Development Unit, Dept. of Professional &
                        Human Studies, Bretton Hall College of Higher Education, West Bretton,
                        Wakefield WF4 4LG

HALL, Nigel   The Emergence of Literacy   Hodder & Stoughton (1987)

HARRIS, John &   Reading Children's Writing:
WILKINSON, Jeff (eds)   a linguistic view, (see especially ch. 7 and 9)   Allen & Unwin (1986)

HOULTON, David   All Our Languages   Edward Arnold (1985)

INNER LONDON   Stories for the Multi-lingual Classroom   Harcourt, Brace, Jovanovich.
EDUCATION
AUTHORITY

KAY. D. & HARRIS, F.   Writing Development 9-13   Rotherham LEA (1981)

NATIONAL WRITING   Becoming a Writer   Nelson (1989)
PROJECT   Audiences for writing

NEWMAN, Judith   The Craft of Children's Writing   Scholastic Publications (1984)

PETERS, Margaret   Spelling Caught or Taught   Routledge (1985)

OPEN UNIVERSITY   Every Child's Language (resources pack with audio-tape KT 420.7)

RABAN, Bridie(ed)   Practical Ways to Teach Writing   Ward Lock (1985)

SASSOON, Rosemary   The Practical Guide to Children's Handwriting   Thames & Hudson (1983)

SMITH, Frank   Writing & the Writer   Heinemann (1982)

TORBE, Mike   Teaching Spelling   Ward Lock Educational (1977)

TEMPLE, C.A.,   The Beginnings of Writing   Allyn & Bacon (1982)
NATHAN,Ruth G. &
BURRIS, Nancy A.

CHILDREN'S WRITING
In the Nursery

[child's handwriting/scribbles]

What a lovely Christmas you had!

Sarah already has communicated intent. "Here's a letter to you - it's all about what I got for Christmas," she said to her teacher. After a further few minutes at the writing corner, she reappeared, saying "Do you know Away in a Manger? I've written it for you," and promptly sang it, reading from the 'words' below.

[child's handwriting/scribbles]

Fancy — you know the whole song!

Debbie also knows she can communicate by making marks on paper and she is showing awareness of the English alphabetic system.

Is it a message for me?
(Nods) It says "Hello"

HOTHOTHOTHOTHO

Having taken great care in first choosing her writing implement, Mahmoona then reveals developing spatial awareness and a sense of patterning in her writing.

Usman's first attempt at the writing table. He wrote, without hesitation, from right to left and from top to bottom. Like Mahmoona, Usman's first language is Urdu.

In the Infants

Matthew can write most of the letters in his name and he uses them randomly.

I ht eo

MtoW oM

IotoWMo

OotMOM

I stay inside too
when it's raining.

Thomas is beginning to associate letters with sounds "I liked helping," he says.

6.289

I llevheehE

Yes you were a good help to me on
friday

Sarah has a real purpose for writing. She takes risks and makes alterations with confidence.

Dear. mrs Redfarm
I wold like to now
when the Shcool. fear
is becoes I wanb
to go I hope the
class and shcool are
haveing a good time
and I miss you all
very mash. I hope
miss Hatford and miss.
Haban. and miss ydag
are ~~all~~ and miss piqe.
and all athers are
heveing a good time.
I will come and
see you sooh.
I hope mrs mather
and mrs woodcoke are
allright: Iy hard thet
mrs mather is back
from hareing a
baby my sister

carla missis the.
nasary bow and
of cors. Jodie.
and ofcors Jodie
is a little pest
at home and I
hope you have
a good christmas.
Ill send you a card
at christmas. I miss
you very very very
very mash. are
now shcool is
calld west wood Kash
Jonay shcool. I hope
you all have a
very very very
good time. Lots
of love from
Sarah Jodie xxx
mum dad xxxx
Carla Baker xxxx

By co-operating in a brainstorming session, a group of seven year olds have collected ideas that will provide a framework for writing.

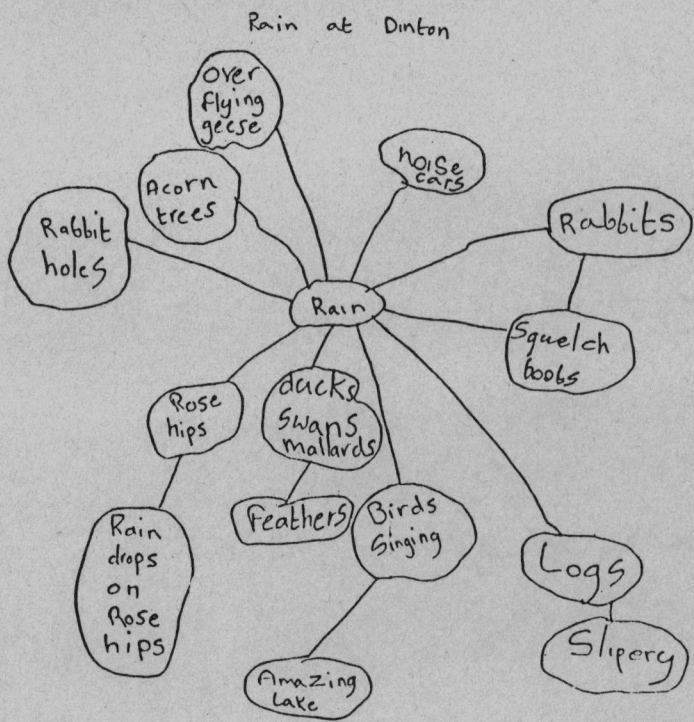

Rain at Dinton

In the Juniors

First Draft

I Like (STMPS) becues when I grw
I (miat) (becum Famus). and I have
a big (STMP) Book and I Like (sic)
them in the Book. and my
mummy (h ellp) me to (sic) them II
and every weekend I (by) ~some~ STMP:
and they cost 50P or~~(£0.00)~~ ~from 50p – £3.00.~ £1·00 of. E
or £2·00 of £2·50 of £3·00.

Points from consultation with the teacher.

cleting stmp
goieen siwink
waeing tv
goisen to a culb

clehia - collecting
stmps - stamps
mint - might
gwor - grow
sik - sticking
helles 'helps'
BU - buy

Final Draft

.Lucy
I Like stamps because when I grow up I
might become Famous. I have got a big
stamp book. My mummy helps me to stick
them in: and every weekend I by some
stamps From 50p — £3·00.

Encouraging the use of community languages in the classroom can be an important factor in developing bilingual children's sense of authorship.

The snake who hid in his hole.
I am going to tell you a story
about a snake. The snake escaped from a field
on the farm. My cousin came to my house and
then lots of people came to try to kill
the snake, but the snake escaped down
his hole. Then my cousin got a spade and
Killed the snake. Then he tricked my little
sister........

ایک سانپ جو اپنے بل میں چھپ گیا
میں آپ کو ایک کہانی بتاؤں گا ایک سانپ کی۔ ایک سانپ
[Urdu text]
[Urdu text]
[Urdu text]
[Urdu text]
[Urdu text]
[Urdu text]
[Urdu text]
[Urdu text]
[Urdu text]
[Urdu text]
[Urdu text]
[Urdu text]
[Urdu text]
ختم شد
زیں لغا

First draft showing self-editing techniques.

Looking After A Dog

First of all when you get a ~~dog~~ a (puppy) you have (doyls to get some (jabs) before you take it the dog out for a walk and you must have one jab every year. To (prtest) the dog from (desed). Then it is best to feed your dog regular at a (regle) time about six o'clock every (mist night 2 and don't give the dog too much (goodies) or it the dog will be fat and not fit It is best to give the dog two walks a day 3 be for you go to work and when you get back. It is good to take your dog for a run every week end in a (loke) woody stire a and you must (shoe (howls answer, bose and make shore he can't the dog (anlse) to his name chase and dosen not (chese) after other dogs 4.

(margin notes: puppy, jabs, protect, disease, regular, goodies, labal, stire, answer, bose, chase)

dogs and it (changs) your ~~lil it~~ life because you have to get (ojir home first to feed the dog then.
2 and if you do not give it (meles) the dog will die.
3 because if you don't the dog might tam on you these are the best time to do it.
4 ~~aus~~ your dog might have to be put down.

(margin notes: meds)

Christopher and his teacher redrafted together during a consultation, then he produced his final draft on his own.

Looking After A Dog

When you first get a puppy it changes your life. You have to get home early to feed the dog. The dog has to get some jabs before you take it out for a walk. It must have one jab every year. To protect the dog from disease and fleas. It is best to feed your dog at a regular time, about six o'clock every night. If you do not give it meals the dog will die. But if you give the dog too many goodies the dog will be fat and unfit. It is

It is best to give the dog two walks a day because, if you don't the dog might tam on you and the dog will not have a chance to go to the toilet. The best times to do it are before you go to work and when you get back.

It is good to take your dog for a run every week end in a local wood. You must show who is boss and make sure the dog answers to his name and dosen't chase after other dogs because your dog might have to be put down.

ALSO FROM TRENTHAM BOOKS

LOOKING INTO LANGUAGE: DIVERSITY IN THE CLASSROOM
Audrey Gregory and Norah Woollard

The Swann report has argued that bilingualism is a rich source for the bilingual child and for the classroom and that it should be recognised as such instead of being treated as a deficit requiring remedial attention. Practical ways of implementing Swann's recommendations on bilingualism in the primary classroom are described in detail in this splendid compilation that was originally published by Berkshire Education Authority.

"It made me itch to try out some of the ideas."
Bookquest

"Very readable and professional looking . . . Well illustrated by black and white drawings which could serve as a model to other LEA resource producers."
Dragon's Teeth

1985. Reprinted 1987, 1988, 1989
ISBN 0 948080 04 3
Price £6.50, 109 pages, A4

Trentham Books Limited
Unit 13/14, Trent Trading Park,
Botteslow Street, Hanley,
Stoke-on-Trent, Staffordshire ST1 3LY